My United States
Kansas

JOSH GREGORY

Children's Press®
An Imprint of Scholastic Inc.

Content Consultant

James Wolfinger, PhD, Associate Dean and Professor
College of Education, DePaul University, Chicago, Illinois

Library of Congress Cataloging-in-Publication Data
Names: Gregory, Josh, author.
Title: Kansas / by Josh Gregory.
Description: New York, NY : Children's Press, an imprint of Scholastic Inc., 2018. | Series: A true book | Includes
    bibliographical references and index.
Identifiers: LCCN 2017051834 | ISBN 9780531235607 (library binding) | ISBN 9780531250792 (pbk.)
Subjects: LCSH: Kansas—Juvenile literature.
Classification: LCC F681.3 .G74 2018 | DDC 978.1—dc23
LC record available at https://lccn.loc.gov/2017051834

Photographs ©: cover: Rawpixel/iStockphoto; back cover bottom: Andy Sacks/Getty Images; back cover ribbon: AliceLiddelle/
Getty Images; 3 bottom: Americanspirit/Dreamstime; 3 map: Jim McMahon/Mapman ®; 4 right: Antagain/iStockphoto; 4 left:
photographybyJHWilliams/iStockphoto; 5 top: Jamie Squire/Getty Images; 5 bottom: tomofbluesprings/iStockphoto; 6 inset:
Bill Bachmann/Alamy Images; 7 center: Gerrit Vyn/Minden Pictures; 7 bottom: Danita Delimont/Alamy Images; 7 top: Walter
Arce/Dreamstime; 8-9: luchschen/iStockphoto; 11: TommyBrison/Shutterstock; 12: marekuliasz/Shutterstock; 13: Jim Reed/
Getty Images; 14: tomofbluesprings/iStockphoto; 15: Wendy Shattil/Alamy Images; 16-17: Jeff Zehnder/Shutterstock; 19:
JSantiagoPhoto/iStockphoto; 20: Teguh Mujiono/Shutterstock; 22 left: Alan Cotton/Alamy Images; 22 right: grebeshkovmaxim/
Shutterstock; 23 top left: najin/iStockphoto; 23 bottom right: Juniors Bildarchiv GmbH/Alamy Images; 23 top right: Antagain/
iStockphoto; 23 center left: DNY59/iStockphoto; 23 bottom left: AmbientIdeas/iStockphoto; 23 center right: photographyby-
JHWilliams/iStockphoto; 24-25: dieKleinert/Alamy Images; 27: Library of Congress; 29: Ed Vebell/Getty Images; 30 bottom:
dieKleinert/Alamy Images; 30 top: Library of Congress; 31 top left: Alan Cotton/Alamy Images; 31 top right: Everett Historical/
Shutterstock; 31 bottom: Ed Vebell/Getty Images; 32: Everett Historical/Shutterstock; 33: Science & Society Picture Library/Getty
Images; 34-35: National Geographic Creative/Alamy Images; 36: Peter G. Aiken/Getty Images; 37: National Geographic Creative/
Alamy Images; 38: Grant Heilman Photography/Alamy Images; 39: KSwinicki/iStockphoto; 40 inset: Michelle Arnold/EyeEm/
Getty Images; 40 background: PepitoPhotos/Getty Images; 41: Nick Krug/AP Images; 42 top left: Evening Standard/Getty Images;
42 top right: Underwood Archives/Getty Images; 42 bottom left: Ulf Andersen/Getty Images; 42 center right: Bettmann/Getty
Images; 42 bottom right: William Gottlieb/Getty Images; 43 top left: Michael Caulfield/Getty Images; 43 top right: Cindy Ord/
Getty Images; 43 center left: Franco Origlia/Getty Images; 43 center right: Jesse Grant/Getty Images; 43 bottom left: Joe Robbins/
Getty Images; 43 bottom center: Debra L Rothenberg/Getty Images; 43 bottom right: Jared Siskin/Getty Images; 44 top: Wspin/
Shutterstock; 44 bottom right: Jamie Squire/Getty Images; 44 bottom left: Michael Hudson/Alamy Images; 45 center: Mike
Theiss/Getty Images; 45 top right: Kansas City Star/Getty Images; 45 top left: James R. Martin/Shutterstock; 45 bottom: Alan
Cotton/Alamy Images.

Maps by Map Hero, Inc.

**Front cover: Monument Rocks
National Landmark**

Back cover: Harvesting alfalfa

Welcome to Kansas

Key Facts

Capital: Topeka

Estimated population as of 2017: 2,913,123

Nickname: Sunflower State

Biggest cities: Wichita, Overland Park, Kansas City

UNITED STATES

Kansas

Find the Truth!

Everything you are about to read is true *except* for one of the sentences on this page.

Which one is **TRUE**?

T or F Kansas has a large population of German Americans.

T or F The United States purchased Kansas from Spain.

KANSAS

DBL TRBL

Find the answers in this book.

Contents

THE **BIG** TRUTH!

Honeybee

What Represents Kansas?

Western
meadowlark

4

University of
Kansas Jayhawks

3 History

How did Kansas become
the state it is today?

4 Culture

What do Kansans do for work and fun?

Sunflowers

This Is Kansas!

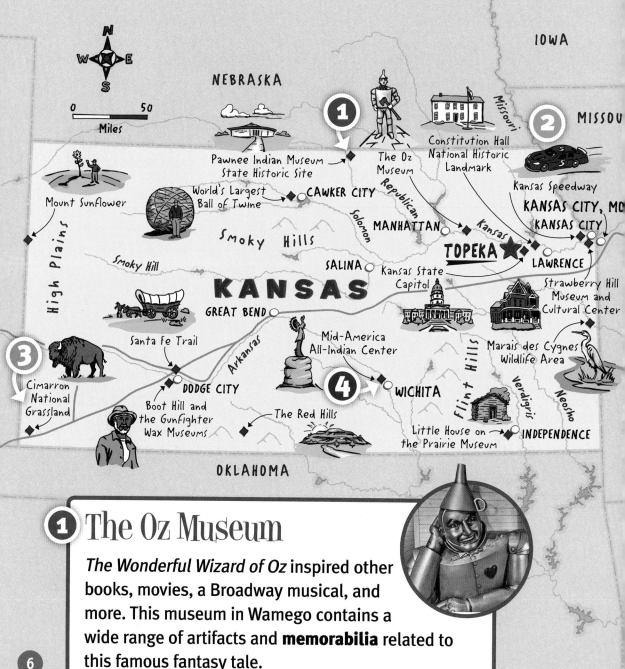

IOWA

NEBRASKA

1 The Oz Museum

Pawnee Indian Museum State Historic Site

Constitution Hall National Historic Landmark

2 MISSOU

Kansas Speedway

KANSAS CITY, MO

KANSAS CITY

World's Largest Ball of Twine

CAWKER CITY

Republican

Missouri

Mount Sunflower

Smoky Hills

MANHATTAN

Kansas

High Plains

Smoky Hill

Solomon

TOPEKA ★

LAWRENCE

SALINA

Kansas State Capitol

Strawberry Hill Museum and Cultural Center

KANSAS

GREAT BEND

Santa Fe Trail

Arkansas

Mid-America All-Indian Center

Marais des Cygnes Wildlife Area

Flint Hills

3

Cimarron National Grassland

DODGE CITY

Boot Hill and the Gunfighter Wax Museums

4 → WICHITA

The Red Hills

Little House on → the Prairie Museum

Verdigris

Neosho

INDEPENDENCE

OKLAHOMA

0 — 50
Miles

1 The Oz Museum

The Wonderful Wizard of Oz inspired other books, movies, a Broadway musical, and more. This museum in Wamego contains a wide range of artifacts and **memorabilia** related to this famous fantasy tale.

ILLINOIS INDIANA

② Kansas Speedway

On race weekends, tens of thousands of fans pack this speedway to watch the world's top race car drivers compete. The speedway has hosted several annual NASCAR events since 2001.

③ Cimarron National Grassland

Located in southwestern Kansas, this sprawling 108,175-acre (43,777-hectare) grassland is home to a huge variety of plants and wildlife. Visitors love hiking, camping, or just driving through to admire the scenery.

MISSOURI

TENNESSEE

④ Mid-America All-Indian Center

This museum in Wichita is dedicated to preserving the culture and art of Kansas's Native American peoples. Art and history exhibits are always on display. The museum also offers art classes and hosts special events.

ARKANSAS

MISSISSIPPI

ALABAMA

About 20 percent of all the wheat grown in the United States comes from Kansas.

CHAPTER 1

Land and Wildlife

From north to south and east to west, the state of Kansas lies almost exactly in the center of the United States. It is a place where cows graze on tall grass under the shining sun. Rivers wind around gently sloping hills. A pleasant breeze sends waves across a golden wheat field. With its wide-open spaces, seemingly endless expanses of farmland, and charming small towns, Kansas is truly the heartland of America.

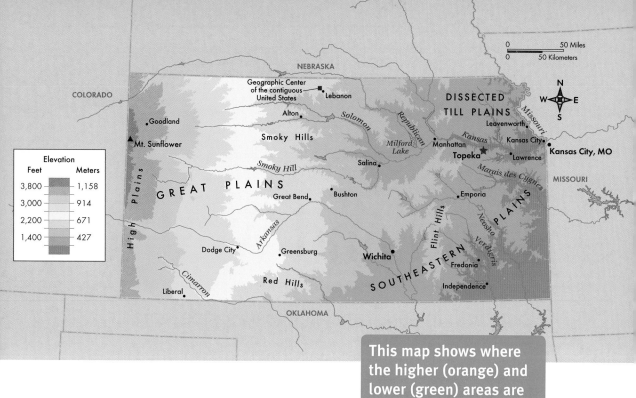

 — map content:

NEBRASKA

COLORADO

50 Miles
50 Kilometers

Geographic Center
of the contiguous
United States · Lebanon

DISSECTED
TILL PLAINS

Leavenworth

N
W · E
S

Alton
Goodland
Solomon
Republican
Kansas
Kansas City
Milford Manhattan
Lake
Topeka ★ Lawrence
Kansas City, MO

Mt. Sunflower

Smoky Hills

Salina

MISSOURI

Elevation

Feet	Meters
3,800	1,158
3,000	914
2,200	671
1,400	427

Smoky Hill

Marais des Cygnes

High Plains

GREAT PLAINS

Great Bend
Bushton
Emporia

Arkansas

Flint Hills
Neosho
Verdigris
PLAINS

Dodge City
Greensburg
Wichita

Cimarron

Red Hills
Fredonia

SOUTHEASTERN

Liberal
Independence

OKLAHOMA

This map shows where the higher (orange) and lower (green) areas are in Kansas.

Geography

Kansas has an almost perfectly rectangular shape. The only exception is its jagged northeastern corner, which follows the path of the Missouri River. Each of Kansas's four sides borders a single state. Nebraska is to the north, Missouri to the east, Oklahoma to the south, and Colorado to the west. Within these borders lies a variety of beautiful landscapes.

Tallgrass Prairie National Preserve

One of the state's most unique natural environments can be found in Tallgrass **Prairie** National Preserve. The preserve protects about 11,000 acres (4,452 ha) of tallgrass prairie **ecosystem** in the Flint Hills region of eastern Kansas. Tallgrass prairie once covered about 170 million acres (68.8 million ha) of North America. As more people moved to the region in the 1800s and 1900s, however, almost all of this land became farms and towns. Today, most of the remaining tallgrass prairie land is in Kansas.

The western two-thirds of Kansas are a part of the country's enormous Great Plains region. It is mostly flat, with some gentle hills, and covered in short grasses. But there are also sandy dunes and wet marshes here.

Eastern Kansas has a more varied landscape. Here, there are plenty of rivers, rolling green hills, forests, and rock formations.

Castle Rock is a limestone formation that rises up from the prairie of western Kansas.

MAXIMUM TEMPERATURE
121°F

MINIMUM TEMPERATURE
-40°F

Professional storm chasers observe a tornado in Kansas's Greeley County.

SEVERE WEATHER RESEARCH UNIT #2

Climate

Kansas residents enjoy warm, sunny summers. Winters are cold, with plenty of snow. Kansas is also a very windy place. On a hot summer day, the breeze can be pleasant. Sometimes, however, the winds can turn destructive. As part of the "Tornado Alley" region, Kansas is hit by dozens of tornadoes each year. Bringing winds up to 300 miles (483 kilometers) per hour, these storms can destroy buildings and send cars flying through the air.

Plants

With so much grass growing everywhere, it might seem at first like Kansas doesn't have a wide range of plant life. There is more variety, however, than meets the eye. Hundreds of different grass species grow across the state. Kansas also has many colorful wildflowers. Perhaps most striking is the giant yellow sunflower, the official state flower. In eastern Kansas's forests, maples, oaks, and many other kinds of trees rise high above the ground.

About 65,500 acres (26,507 ha) of farmland in Kansas are used to grow sunflowers.

Prairie dog tunnels have separate rooms for activities such as sleeping, caring for babies, and going to the bathroom.

Animals

Kansas is full of interesting animals. The grasslands of the Great Plains are the perfect place for large mammals such as cows and buffalo to graze. Underground, prairie dogs scurry through the elaborate tunnel systems they dig. Birds such as turkeys, prairie chickens, and pheasants peck at the ground for seeds, insects, and other tasty treats. Elk and coyotes can be spotted in the state's wooded areas. Several bat species take to the sky after sunset.

The Kansas capitol cost more than three million dollars to build.

CHAPTER 2

Government

When Kansas became a state in 1861, its leaders chose the city of Topeka to serve as their capital. It took a long time, however, for the state government to become settled in its new home. Construction on the capitol did not begin until 1866, and it took about 37 years to finish. Since then, lawmakers from across the state have gathered in this magnificent building to debate how the state is run.

State Government Structure

Kansas's government is organized much like other U.S. state governments. It has three branches. The executive branch is headed by a governor. It carries out state laws by managing a number of programs and agencies. The legislative branch includes a Senate and a House of Representatives. It creates new laws. Finally, the judicial branch is made up of the state's court system. It interprets state laws by hearing and ruling on court cases.

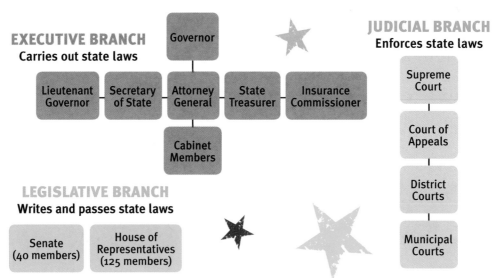

KANSAS'S STATE GOVERNMENT

EXECUTIVE BRANCH
Carries out state laws

Governor

Lieutenant Governor · Secretary of State · Attorney General · State Treasurer · Insurance Commissioner

Cabinet Members

LEGISLATIVE BRANCH
Writes and passes state laws

Senate (40 members) · House of Representatives (125 members)

JUDICIAL BRANCH
Enforces state laws

Supreme Court

Court of Appeals

District Courts

Municipal Courts

Many services, such as fire departments, are provided by local governments rather than the Kansas state government.

A Blueprint for Government

As part of the process to become a state, Kansas **Territory** lawmakers had to create a **constitution**. This document then had to be approved by the U.S. Congress. It took territory lawmakers four tries to create a constitution that Congress approved. This successful document continues to serve as the basis of the state government today. It outlines the structure of the state government, the process for creating new laws, how taxes are collected, and much more.

Kansas in the National Government

Each state elects officials to represent it in the U.S. Congress. Like every state, Kansas has two senators. The U.S. House of Representatives relies on a state's population to determine its numbers. Kansas has four representatives in the House.

Every four years, states vote on the next U.S. president. Each state is granted a number of electoral votes based on its number of members in Congress. With two senators and four representatives, Kansas has six electoral votes.

2 senators and 4 representatives

6 electoral votes

With six electoral votes, Kansas's voice in presidential elections is below average compared to other states.

The People of Kansas

Elected officials in Kansas represent a population with a range of interests, lifestyles, and backgrounds.

Ethnicity (2016 estimates)

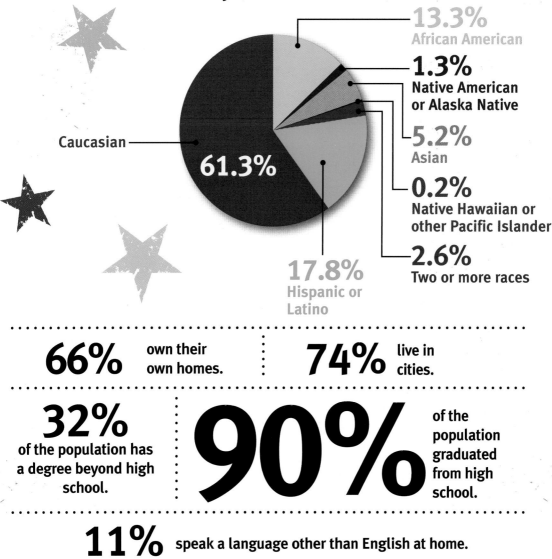

13.3%
African American

1.3%
Native American or Alaska Native

5.2%
Asian

0.2%
Native Hawaiian or other Pacific Islander

2.6%
Two or more races

Caucasian

61.3%

17.8%
Hispanic or Latino

66% own their own homes.

74% live in cities.

32% of the population has a degree beyond high school.

90% of the population graduated from high school.

11% speak a language other than English at home.

What Represents Kansas?

States choose specific animals, plants, and objects to represent the values and characteristics of the land and its people. Find out why these symbols were chosen to represent Kansas or discover surprising curiosities about them.

Seal

Kansas's seal features images that relate to the state's history. They include a farmer plowing his field, a riverboat, Native Americans hunting bison, and covered wagons crossing the plains. The state motto, "*Ad Astra per Aspera*," is Latin for "To the stars through difficulties." A cluster of 34 stars represents Kansas's position as the 34th state.

Flag

Kansas's flag displays the state seal on a blue field, along with a sunflower, the state flower.

American Bison

STATE ANIMAL

About 20 million bison once roamed the Great Plains. They were an important source of food, clothing, and other valuable materials to Native Americans.

Honeybee

STATE INSECT

This hardworking insect has long provided the people of Kansas with honey and wax.

Western Meadowlark

STATE BIRD

The meadowlark's distinctive song often fills the air during summer in Kansas.

Cottonwood

STATE TREE

This tree is named for the wispy, white seeds it releases into the wind each spring.

Sunflower

STATE FLOWER

As they are growing, these enormous, yellow flowers turn to face the sun as it moves across the sky during the day.

Ornate Box Turtle

STATE REPTILE

Common throughout Kansas, this turtle can live up to 50 years in the wild.

Mammoths died out in Kansas by about 8000 BCE.

CHAPTER 3

History

Thousands of years ago, huge animals such as mammoths and mastodons roamed the Great Plains. These now-extinct creatures lived alongside bison and other species that are still there today. In about 10,000 BCE, **nomadic** people arrived in the area. They hunted the animals of the Great Plains using spears and other handmade weapons. In addition to eating the animals' meat, the hunters made everything from tools to clothing using other animal parts.

Native Americans

Over time, the people of what is now Kansas began settling down. Instead of roaming from place to place in search of animals and plants to eat, they built farms and villages. They constructed their homes from wood, grass, animal skins, and other natural materials. Some people continued to hunt for meat, but they also grew a variety of crops, including pumpkins, corn, and beans.

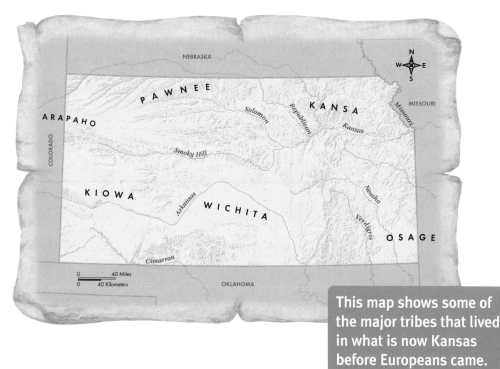

This map shows some of the major tribes that lived in what is now Kansas before Europeans came.

By the 1500s, several different cultures called Kansas home. In the northeast were the Kansa. The Kansa grew a variety of crops, but also sent groups of men and

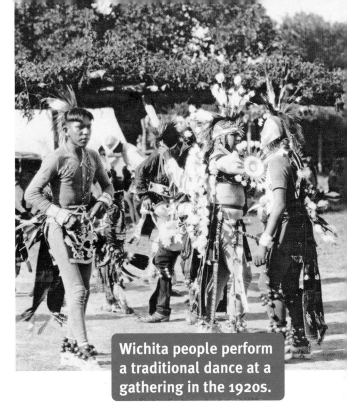

Wichita people perform a traditional dance at a gathering in the 1920s.

women on long hunting trips in the fall. South of them were the Osage people, who led a similar lifestyle. The Pawnee and Wichita people lived farther west. Both spoke a language called Caddoan. Along the western edge of the state were the Arapaho and Kiowa.

Kansas is named after the Kansa people. They were among the first Native Americans in the area to encounter European explorers.

European Settlers

In 1541, Spanish explorers under Francisco Vásquez de Coronado became the first known Europeans to visit Kansas. Their visit was brief. The next Europeans did not arrive until the late 1600s. In 1673, French explorers traveled down the Mississippi River and mapped the surrounding area, including parts of Kansas. Nine years later, explorer René-Robert Cavelier, sieur de La Salle, claimed Kansas for France. It was part of a much larger region he claimed called Louisiana.

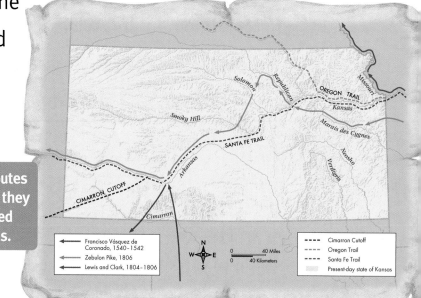

This map shows routes Europeans took as they explored and settled what is now Kansas.

The Lewis and Clark party used poles to push their boat along shallow areas as they traveled along the Missouri River.

In 1803, the United States purchased Louisiana from France. The following year, President Thomas Jefferson sent a team led by Meriwether Lewis and William Clark to explore the area. They arrived in what is now Kansas in June and celebrated the Fourth of July there. Two years later, U.S. Army officer Zebulon Pike met with Pawnee and Osage leaders in Kansas.

The Fight Against Slavery

In 1854, the U.S. government officially created the Kansas Territory. Thousands of Americans and immigrants moved into the area. Almost right away, the new settlers began thinking about statehood. At the time, the debate over **slavery** was a major issue in the country. Some people in Kansas wanted to allow slavery, like the Southern states. Others wanted slavery to be illegal.

Timeline of Kansas Events

10,000 BCE
People come to the Great Plains region for the first time.

1541
Spanish explorer Vásquez de Coronado becomes the first European to visit Kansas.

10,000 BCE → 1500s CE → 1541 → 1803

1500s CE
Native American groups such as the Kansa, Pawnee, and Wichita live in what is now Kansas.

1803
The United States acquires Kansas as part of the Louisiana Purchase.

For years, pro- and anti-slavery groups in Kansas fought over the issue. Finally, on January 29, 1861, Kansas joined the United States as a free state. The anti-slavery movement had won in Kansas. But just three months later, the national debate over slavery launched the Civil War (1861–1865). About 20,000 Kansans joined the fight against the pro-slavery Southern states. They helped win the war and make slavery illegal across the entire country.

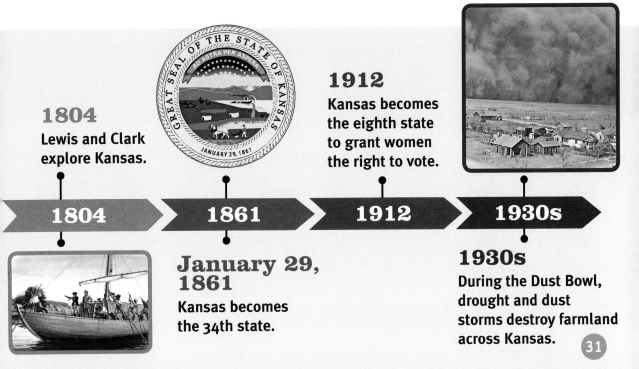

1804
Lewis and Clark explore Kansas.

1912
Kansas becomes the eighth state to grant women the right to vote.

1804 **1861** **1912** **1930s**

January 29, 1861
Kansas becomes the 34th state.

1930s
During the Dust Bowl, drought and dust storms destroy farmland across Kansas.

31

An enormous dust storm swept across the town of Rolla in 1935.

A Growing State

After the war, Kansas experienced rapid expansion. New railroads made it easier to reach the state. Thousands of people came to work on farms, in mines, and at other businesses. Then in the 1930s, a long **drought** turned Kansas's rich farmland into a dusty wasteland. It took years to recover.

In the 1950s, Kansas played a major role in the civil rights movement. A lawsuit against the Topeka Board of Education led to a U.S. Supreme Court decision declaring it illegal for public schools to be **segregated**.

Dwight D. Eisenhower

Though born in Texas, Dwight D. Eisenhower grew up in Abilene, Kansas. During World War II (1939–1945), Eisenhower led U.S. forces and their allies to victory in Europe. His popularity as a military leader helped him win a landslide victory when he ran for president in 1952. Ike, as he was known, served two terms in office. During this time, he worked hard to maintain peace around the world. He became one of the most widely liked presidents in history.

More than 300,000 people attend the Kansas State Fair each year.

CHAPTER 4

Culture

From the sparsely populated western half of the state to the cities in the east, Kansas is full of things to do and see. With their diverse populations and wealth of museums, theaters, and other attractions, big cities such as Topeka and Kansas City are cultural centers. Even the state's smallest towns offer plenty of celebrations and beautiful natural scenery.

On the Court

Kansans love to play and watch their favorite sports. Fans cheer on the Sporting Kansas City pro soccer team. The state also has a rich basketball history. The University of Kansas Jayhawks basketball team was founded in 1898. This makes it one of the world's oldest basketball teams. The

Jayhawks' first coach was James Naismith, the game's inventor. The team has long been a powerhouse of college basketball, winning many championships over its long history.

Kansas basketball fans have to choose a side when the University of Kansas Jayhawks face off against the Kansas State University Wildcats.

Spectators cheer during a pig race at the Kansas State Fair.

Fairs and Festivals

Kansas has a large population of German Americans. Because of this, many towns across the state hold Oktoberfests each fall. At these celebrations, people enjoy traditional German food, music, and more. Another popular event is the Kansas State Fair. Each September, the fair draws hundreds of thousands of people to the town of Hutchinson. They celebrate Kansas agriculture, enjoy live entertainment and rides, eat tasty food, and take part in other fun activities.

A thresher is a machine used to separate the seeds of grain plants from stalks and husks.

Kansas at Work

Kansans work in many different jobs. One of the state's biggest industries is agriculture. Farmers grow huge amounts of wheat, corn, sunflowers, and many other crops. Ranchers raise cows, pigs, and other livestock. Thousands of other Kansans work in the aircraft industry, building planes. Others assemble cars, electronics, and other products in factories. Many Kansans work in service jobs, such as teachers, doctors, and restaurant employees.

About one-fourth of Kansas's electricity comes from wind. This amount is expected to increase over time.

A Powerful State

Kansas has a wealth of resources for generating energy. Throughout the 20th century, the state was a major source of coal. The mining industry provided many jobs to Kansans. The coal industry has been shrinking, however, as people turn to cleaner energy sources. Luckily for Kansas, its wide-open plains and plentiful sunshine make it the perfect place to capture wind and solar power. Jobs related to coal will eventually be replaced with jobs in these alternative energies.

Kansas Cuisine

Kansans love country-style home cooking. Many families have their own recipes for classic dishes such as fried chicken and apple pie. People also bake a lot of bread, often using flour from the wheat that is grown across the state. Barbecue is a big deal in Kansas, too. Meats of all kinds are seasoned, slow-roasted, and coated in tangy sauce.

Kansas City BBQ Sauce

Ask an adult to help you!

You can dip everything from french fries to chicken in this sweet, spicy sauce.

Ingredients

2 tablespoons butter
1 cup minced onions
6 cloves garlic, minced
2 tablespoons tomato paste
2 cups ketchup
2 tablespoons yellow mustard

1 tablespoon chili powder
$1/2$ teaspoon cayenne pepper
1 teaspoon black pepper
$1/4$ cup molasses
$1/4$ cup dark brown sugar
$1/2$ cup apple cider vinegar

Directions

Melt the butter in a pan over medium heat. Add the onions and garlic and cook until soft. Add the rest of the ingredients and bring the sauce to a simmer. Cook for about 30 minutes, stirring often.

Lawrence residents paint a colorful street mural as part of a local Earth Day celebration in 2016.

The Heart of the Country

Each year on January 29, Kansas's birthday, the state's residents celebrate Kansas Day. Local museums offer special events to teach people about state history, and small towns hold potlucks. People sing "Home on the Range," the official state song. Kansans are proud of where they live, and they love their state. Local traditions, friendly people, and gorgeous landscapes make Kansas an incredible place for residents and visitors alike. ★

Famous People

Amelia Earhart

(1897–1937?) became the first woman to complete a solo airplane flight across the Atlantic Ocean in 1928. She later disappeared over the Pacific Ocean while attempting to fly around the world. Bones that possibly belonged to Earhart were later discovered on an island. She was a native of Atchison.

Langston Hughes

(1902–1967) was a writer and social activist who helped lead the Harlem Renaissance arts movement in the 1920s. He grew up in Lawrence.

William S. Burroughs

(1914–1997) was a writer and artist who played a major role in the Beat Generation literary movement. He was a longtime resident of Lawrence.

Gwendolyn Brooks

(1917–2000) was a poet whose 1949 book *Annie Allen* made her the first African American to win a Pulitzer Prize. She was born in Topeka.

Charlie Parker

(1920–1955) was a saxophonist who helped pioneer the bebop style of jazz music. Nicknamed "Bird," he was born in Kansas City.

Dennis Hopper

(1936–2010) was an actor, filmmaker, photographer, and artist who became famous for his work in such films as *Easy Rider* and *Apocalypse Now*. He was born in Dodge City.

Kirstie Alley

(1951–) is an award-winning actor who has appeared in many films and TV series. She is from Wichita.

Annette Bening

(1958–) is an Academy Award–nominated actor who has received widespread acclaim for her work in such films as *The Kids Are All Right*. She is from Topeka.

Melissa Etheridge

(1961–) is a Grammy Award–winning singer-songwriter and guitarist. She was born and raised in Leavenworth.

Barry Sanders

(1968–) is a former professional football star whose 10 seasons with the Detroit Lions earned him a place in the Pro Football Hall of Fame. He was born and raised in Wichita.

Paul Rudd

(1969–) is an actor and comedian who has appeared in such films as *Ant-Man*. He grew up in Overland Park and attended the University of Kansas.

Janelle Monáe

(1985–) is a Grammy-nominated singer-songwriter. She has also starred in such films as *Moonlight* and *Hidden Figures*. She is from Kansas City.

Did You Know That ...

Kansas City, located on the eastern border of Kansas, is actually two cities. One is Kansas City, Kansas. The other is Kansas City, Missouri. The larger section is in Missouri, but the Kansas part is still one of the biggest cities in Kansas.

Smith County, in northern Kansas, contains the exact center point of the lower 48 United States.

When the people of the Kansas Territory were fighting over whether Kansas should be a free state, anti-slavery groups called themselves jayhawks. This nickname represented the idea that they were noisy like blue jays, but with the intelligence of hawks. Today, Kansas is sometimes called the Jayhawk State. The University of Kansas sports teams are also called the Jayhawks.

The Pizza Hut restaurant chain was founded in Wichita in 1958.

The people of Argonia, Kansas, elected Susanna Madora Salter as their mayor in 1887. Salter was the first woman mayor in U.S. history.

Kansas is home to the world's largest ball of twine. Located in Cawker City, people have been adding twine to it for more than 60 years. Today, it weighs about 20,000 pounds (9,072 kilograms) and measures about 42 feet (13 meters) around.

Did you find the truth?

T Kansas has a large population of German Americans.

F The United States purchased Kansas from Spain.

Resources

Books

Bailer, Darice. *What's Great About Kansas?* Minneapolis: Lerner Publications, 2016.

Cannarella, Deborah. *Kansas.* New York: Children's Press, 2015.

Rozett, Louise (ed.). *Fast Facts About the 50 States: Plus Puerto Rico and Washington, D.C.* New York: Children's Press, 2010.

Warren, Andrea. *The Boy Who Became Buffalo Bill: Growing Up Billy Cody in Bleeding Kansas.* New York: Two Lions, 2015.

Visit this Scholastic website for more information on Kansas:
★ www.factsfornow.scholastic.com
Enter the keyword **Kansas**

Important Words

constitution (kahn-stih-TOO-shuhn) the basic laws of a country or state that detail the rights of the people and the power of the government

drought (DROUT) a long period without rain

ecosystem (EE-koh-sis-tuhm) all the living things in a place and their relation to their environment

memorabilia (mem-ur-uh-BEE-lee-uh) objects that are kept because of their relationship to a specific topic or event

nomadic (noh-MAD-ik) traveling from place to place instead of living in the same place all the time

prairie (PRAIR-ee) a large area of flat or rolling grassland with few or no trees

segregated (SEG-ruh-gay-tid) separated or kept apart

slavery (SLAY-vur-ee) the system in which a person may be owned and thought of as property

territory (TER-uh-tor-ee) a part of the United States that is not within any state but has its own legislature

Index

Page numbers in **bold** indicate illustrations.

About the Author

Josh Gregory is the author of more than 125 books for kids. He has written about everything from animals to technology to history. A graduate of the University of Missouri–Columbia, he currently lives in Chicago, Illinois.